## DATE DUE

|  |  |  |  |
|---|---|---|---|
|  |  |  |  |
|  |  |  |  |
|  |  |  |  |
|  |  |  |  |
|  |  |  |  |
|  |  |  |  |
|  |  |  |  |
|  |  |  |  |
|  |  |  |  |
|  |  |  |  |
|  |  |  |  |
|  |  |  |  |
|  |  |  |  |

PEOPLE
IN THE NEWS

# John Grisham

931
GRi

Lucent Books, San Diego, CA

Titles in the People in the News series include:

PEOPLE
IN THE NEWS

# John Grisham

by Robyn M. Weaver

Lucent Books, San Diego, CA

Library of Congress Cataloging-in-Publication Data

Weaver, Robyn.
  John Grisham / by Robyn M. Weaver.
    p. cm. — (People in the news)
  Includes bibliographical references and index.
  Summary: Discusses the life, career, and influence of the popular writer of legal thrillers.
  ISBN 1-56006-530-3 (alk. paper)
  1. Grisham, John—Juvenile literature. 2. Legal stories, American —History and criticism—Juvenile literature. 3. Novelists, American—20th century—Biography—Juvenile literature.
  [1. Grisham, John. 2. Authors, American.] I. Title. II. Series: People in the news (San Diego, Calif.)
PS3557.R5355Z96   1999
813'.54—dc21
[B]                                                           99-14325
                                                                 CIP
                                                                  AC

Copyright © 1999 by Lucent Books, Inc.
P.O. Box 289011
San Diego, CA 92198-9011
Printed in the U.S.A.

*Acknowledgements*

The author would like to thank the following people for their generous help in gathering information to include in this book: Dr. Donald Zacharias, president emeritus, Mississippi State University, for his southern charm, intelligence, and encouragement; Sheila Coleman with the John Grisham Room at MSU's Mitchell Memorial Library for her unending patience and good-natured hospitality; Betty Self for her smiling self at MSU special collections reading room desk; Mattie Sink for her well-organized boxes of Grisham material in the special collections department; Scott Ross, for his time and unique contributions; and Penny, for her willingness to tend to the many questions and details necessary for the accuracy of this book.

*For all readers brave enough to admit they are not ashamed to enjoy a good read.*

# Table of Contents

# Foreword

$F$AME AND CELEBRITY are alluring. People are drawn to those who walk in fame's spotlight, whether they are known for great accomplishments or for notorious deeds. The lives of the famous pique public interest and attract attention, perhaps because their experiences seem in some ways so different from, yet in other ways so similar to, our own.

Newspapers, magazines, and television regularly capitalize on this fascination with celebrity by running profiles of famous people. For example, television programs such as *Entertainment Tonight* devote all of their programming to stories about entertainment and entertainers. Magazines such as *People* fill their pages with stories of the private lives of famous people. Even newspapers, newsmagazines, and television news frequently delve into the lives of well-known personalities. Despite the number of articles and programs, few provide more than a superficial glimpse at their subjects.

Lucent's People in the News series offers young readers a deeper look into the lives of today's newsmakers, the influences that have shaped them, and the impact they have had in their fields of endeavor and on other people's lives. The subjects of the series hail from many disciplines and walks of life. They include authors, musicians, athletes, political leaders, entertainers, entrepreneurs, and others who have made a mark on modern life and who, in many cases, will continue to do so for years to come.

These biographies are more than factual chronicles. Each book emphasizes the contributions, accomplishments, or deeds that have brought fame or notoriety to the individual and shows how that person has influenced modern life. Authors portray their subjects in a realistic, unsentimental light. For example, Bill Gates—the cofounder and chief executive officer of the software giant Microsoft—has been instrumental in making personal computers the most vital tool of the modern age. Few dispute his business savvy, his perseverance, or his technical expertise, yet critics say he is ruthless in his dealings with competitors and driven more by his desire to maintain Microsoft's dominance in the computer industry than by an interest in furthering technology.

In these books, young readers will encounter inspiring stories about real people who achieved success despite enormous obstacles. Oprah Winfrey—the most powerful, most watched, and wealthiest woman on television today—spent the first six years of her life in the care of her grandparents while her unwed mother sought work and a better life elsewhere. Her adolescence was colored by promiscuity, pregnancy at age fourteen, rape, and sexual abuse.

Each author documents and supports his or her work with an array of primary and secondary source quotations taken from diaries, letters, speeches, and interviews. All quotes are footnoted to show readers exactly how and where biographers derive their information and provide guidance for further research. The quotations enliven the text by giving readers eyewitness views of the life and accomplishments of each person covered in the People in the News series.

In addition, each book in the series includes photographs, annotated bibliographies, timelines, and comprehensive indexes. For both the casual reader and the student researcher, the People in the News series offers insight into the lives of today's newsmakers—people who shape the way we live, work, and play in the modern age.

# Introduction

# Superstar Novelist

J OHN GRISHAM'S MILLIONS of loyal readers have made him one of the most recognizable names in the publishing industry. His books have been published in thirty-six different languages, and they consistently land in the number one best-seller slot.

Legal fiction is a category of storytelling that was practically unheard-of before John Grisham entered the publishing scene in 1989. Today legal fiction is nearly as popular as romantic fiction and is one of the most commercially successful categories.

The motion picture industry has also made a great deal of money from John Grisham's stories. Movies based on his novels have starred major Hollywood actors and have introduced Grisham's work to millions of viewers. Ted Conley, a retired head film buyer for Cinemark U.S.A., recalls that when a Grisham movie was due on the market he would try to arrange for it to be shown in as many theaters as possible:

> John Grisham is box-office gold. His novels mean profit for theater owners around the world. From the mega-hit *The Firm* to the mini-hit *The Chamber*, Grisham's stories have a built-in audience. The size of that audience is, of course, enhanced by star power, i.e.: Tom Cruise, Julia Roberts, Susan Sarandon. Even with lesser stars, his films are still box-office winners and eagerly awaited by theater owners everywhere.[1]

Despite his huge success and popularity, John Grisham has tried desperately to remain a quiet, low-key man who avoids public attention and interviews. He also believes that this onslaught of popularity is temporary. At the height of his rise to fame, Grisham told an interviewer:

> I know I'm living a dream. I'm the luckiest person in the world . . . and when it's all over I hope I can look back and say it was a whole lot of fun, but I kept my feet on the ground and I didn't change.[2]

John Grisham may be a celebrity, but he does not enjoy the loss of his privacy. When his family awoke one morning and saw tour buses at the end of their driveway, they knew the time had come to move from Oxford, Mississippi, to a more

*John Grisham has become a celebrity through his writing but tries desperately to stay grounded and retain his privacy.*

secluded area. Today John and his wife, Renee, along with their son, Ty, and daughter, Shea, live in Charlottesville, Virginia. Their new home is far removed from main roads and highways, and the local townspeople respect the family's desire for privacy.

Whether Grisham is writing or talking with friends at a book signing, he usually wears Docker's pants along with a solid-colored button-down shirt, and he only shaves once a week—on Sunday morning (because, he says, the older ladies at church frown on men who have whiskers).

Although he is a faithful Baptist, Grisham has not always portrayed church leaders in an admirable role. In his first novel, *A Time to Kill,* he is candid about the politics within certain churches and the attitudes some of their leaders have regarding money and power. This honesty is what draws many people to Grisham's works. Readers are often able to see parts of themselves in the slightly flawed, ordinary characters who come to life in Grisham novels.

*Although Grisham is a faithful churchgoer, his* A Time to Kill *shows the darker side of church politics and the abuse of power and money.*

Many critics believe that the reader's ability to identify with these characters is what has made Grisham's books so popular; however, others say the legal issues Grisham tackles are broad and often repetitive. He has also endured criticism over a lack of believable characters in his early books. Grisham has answered those reviewers by working hard to write well-rounded people into his more recent novels. Even with the few setbacks, nobody can argue away the success John Grisham has found with his stories, or how marketable that success has become.

Grisham's record-setting book, audio book, and movie sales have altered the pattern of the publishing industry and made his power legendary. For example, book publishers who once hoped to sign numerous writers with smaller loyal audiences now hope to find the one novelist who will become the next John Grisham and generate legions of loyal readers. Likewise, Hollywood producers go to Grisham when they want to discuss movie deals—Grisham does not go to them.

Oddly, though, John Grisham's earliest dreams had nothing to do with writing and everything to do with baseball.

---

# Chapter 1

# Childhood Dreams

J OHN RAY GRISHAM JR. was born on February 8, 1955, in Jonesboro, Arkansas, to strict Southern Baptist parents. His mother was a homemaker, and his father was a construction worker who occasionally farmed when he could find the work. John was the second oldest of the Grishams' five children; and, during his childhood years, his family moved often, depending on where his father sought employment.

## Traveling and Reading

Grisham believes the experience of growing up in such a mobile lifestyle had its merits as well as its inconveniences: "We moved all over from Jonesboro to Crenshaw, MS, to Delhi, LA, to Parkin, AR, to Ripley, [MS], and finally, in 1967, to Southaven [MS]. Though we moved around like gypsies, it was a lot of fun."[3]

The family fell into a pattern of stopping at the local library each time they entered a new town. Grisham's mother strongly believed that her children should not watch too much television. In her opinion, the library trip was a necessity. Moving, not watching a lot of TV, and going to the library are three things that stand out vividly in Grisham's memories of his growing-up years:

> My mother did not believe in television. She thought it was bad, and that was 30 years ago. She believed in books, and we were taught to read early. We moved around a lot when I was a kid, throughout the deep South. We would always go to a new town and go to the library, get our library cards and load up on books.[4]

Despite his mother's encouragement to read, Grisham never considered himself a bookworm. As a child, however, he did have a few favorite stories, such as the Dr. Seuss books, the Hardy Boys series, and Emil and the Detectives. He also read books by Mark Twain and Charles Dickens.

## Baseball Dreams

As a youngster John did not dream of being a writer—he had other dreams. John was not a strong student, and he really only wanted to play sports, especially baseball. Years later, after gaining fame as a writer, Grisham was questioned by an interviewer about his earliest goal in life. He responded:

> To play professional baseball, like every kid, from the time I was six years old until I was 20. It took a long time for the dream to die. It took a long time to realize I didn't have the talent to play, which is always difficult to accept.[5]

*John Grisham signs an autograph for one of his millions of fans.*

## John Grisham's Love of Baseball

John Grisham's love of baseball helped to relax him during his rapid rise to fame. Even during his hectic schedule as a best-selling novelist, he still finds comfort and relaxation in watching the game.

He confided this insight to the graduates he spoke to during the 1992 commencement ceremony at Mississippi State University:

> Not far from here is a dilapidated pickup truck that a friend purchased for a hundred dollars and spray painted by hand. It has no engine, and the tires are flat. Someone installed a few rows of benches, and I am happiest when I'm sitting on top of it watching the Bulldogs play.

With his focus on a future in baseball, John struggled as a student. He was not as interested in learning about math or science as he was about hitting more home runs or throwing a baseball a little faster. Even after graduating from high school, Grisham continued to envision baseball as his career. He also wanted to have a little fun after leaving home:

> I grew up in a very small, close-knit, Southern Baptist family, where everything was off limits. So I couldn't wait to get to college and have some fun. And I did for the first two years. And I regret a lot of it, because my grades were in terrible shape.[6]

Grisham's desire to have fun, plus his passion for baseball, kept him from concentrating on his studies. Together with two roommates who were equally unmotivated, he drifted from one college to another. Grisham always hoped the next college would prove to be the one that would place him in the best slot to make a career out of baseball.

During these first semesters Grisham attended Northwest Junior College and Delta State University, where he changed his major three times. Neither his indecision over college nor his poor grades bothered him, however; he still believed he was going to be discovered by a professional baseball scout.

Then, on a fall day in 1974, Grisham carried his bat to home plate during a game he was playing on the Delta State team. Horrified, he watched a ninety-mile-per-hour fast pitch hurtle straight toward his head. It missed him, but he felt sick from the frightening experience. The next pitch was a little slower, but it was headed straight for his ear. Grisham dove out of the way and was embarrassed to see the ball curve back across the plate for a perfect strike. The next day the team coach called Grisham into his office and dismissed him from the team since he obviously could not hit either a fast ball or a curve ball.

## Dreams Die Hard

Even being kicked off the baseball team did not immediately persuade Grisham to concentrate on his college studies. In a 1991 article in the Mississippi State *Alumnus* magazine, Grisham recalled his outlook after this experience, which eventually led him to Mississippi State University:

> My roommates were restless, and we left Delta State at the end of the semester. One of them wanted to study forestry, so we headed to [Mississippi] State [University]. . . . I had shown not the slightest interest in things academic for the first year and a half of college. Someday, I was certain, someone with vision would pay me a lot of money to play baseball. My grades had started dismally and declined. Who cared? How many Hall of Famers have college degrees?[7]

During Grisham's first day of classes at Mississippi State, he witnessed a heated discussion between two Vietnam War veterans and his professor that changed his view of college. The vets disagreed with opinions the professor voiced, and Grisham enjoyed watching the drama:

> This professor was one of those conservative bomb throwers who thought war was fine as long as someone else was fighting it, and his big mistake was to spout his beliefs before a class which happened to include two Vietnam veterans, one of whom had been wounded and neither of whom appreciated his armchair strategies. A vicious debate erupted as these veterans took him to task. . . . Others smelled blood, and he was soon sur-

*It was Grisham's first day of classes at Mississippi State that led him to take his education more seriously.*

rounded by a nasty pack of angry students. It was wonderful. I was amazed at my class mates who were articulate and prepared and unafraid of attacking a professor.[8]

Although Grisham did not add to the discussion himself, he was impressed with the command of facts and the academic strength his fellow students displayed during the debate. He wanted to be as knowledgeable as his fellow students so he could debate topics with well-thought-out arguments and analytical thinking. This desire provided the incentive he needed to grow up and develop his mind.

## A Student Is Born

From that day on, Grisham began taking his education more seriously. He attended all his classes, listened to his professors, took notes, wrote papers, and studied for tests. He also talked with one of the veterans he had met in that first class, who was an accounting major with good grades. The vet told Grisham

## John Grisham Still Supports MSU

John Grisham is loyal to Mississippi State University and visits often to give commencement speeches. In his 1992 commencement address, Grisham advised graduates to be prepared for surprises that life might have in store for them.

> When I sat out there fifteen years ago, I was rather smug and confident, perhaps even a bit arrogant because I, at the age of twenty-two, had already figured out my life. I had it all planned, and was certain things would fall neatly into place. . . .
>
> In those days, I never thought about writing books. I had never taken a course in creative writing, never studied the craft, never thought about being an author. I was a lawyer, and then I became a lawyer and a legislator. . . .
>
> In 1984, I wrote the first page of the first chapter of *A Time to Kill*. It was a hobby, nothing more. Three years later, I sent the completed manuscript to New York, and immediately wrote the first page of the first chapter of a story that would eventually become *The Firm*. It was just a hobby. . . . If you're sitting out there now with a nice, neat little outline for the next ten years, you'd better be careful. Life may have other plans.

*Grisham delivers the commencement address to a packed house at the spring 1998 graduation ceremony.*

*In college Grisham aimed for a degree in accounting because, although it was one of the hardest to obtain, it offered a secure future.*

that an accounting degree was one of the hardest to obtain but one that would be a great source of income once he graduated.

Grisham took the vet's words to heart and set his sights on an accounting degree. He rose early each morning, studied the *Wall Street Journal*, one of the most popular financial newspapers in the United States, and reviewed his assignments before heading to class. He realized that grades were important to him, and he put all of his energy into finishing college.

In March of his sophomore year, Grisham spent many evenings at the campus baseball field sitting on the wooden bleachers with a thermos of coffee and watching the college teams play. He could not help feeling envious and sad to see the players on the field where he had hoped to be, but it was in this setting that Grisham finally admitted to himself that his future did not lie in professional baseball. He realized that most of the players on that college field would not end up in the major leagues either. He also figured that in a few years most of these players would probably find themselves in the same situation that he was in at that moment—struggling to learn a real career. That realization gave Grisham the strength to leave his boyhood dreams behind him. When college life became too dull, Grisham would write stories. He discovered that this new pastime also helped alleviate the mundane nature of his courses.

As Grisham continued working toward his accounting degree, he looked toward the future, too. After earning his bachelor's degree he planned on going to law school and specializing in tax law. Such a career would allow Grisham to support Renee, the young woman he had been dating during his college years at Mississippi State University.

Many things did turn out as Grisham had planned, including his marriage to Renee. However, his success and fame did not come from playing professional baseball or practicing law: They came from something Grisham had never even considered as a potential career in his early childhood.

John Grisham would make a name for himself by writing books.

----------------------------------------

# Chapter 2

# Building a Legal and Political Career

Aｌｔｈｏｕｇｈ ｈｅ ｎｅｖｅｒ took a creative writing course while he was in college, John Grisham did continue his habits of reading popular authors and writing his own stories. One of his favorite authors throughout high school and college was John Steinbeck. Grisham has mentioned in several interviews that he began his early works in a style similar to Steinbeck's realistic form. Some literary critics confirm that Grisham's style sometimes reflects the stark flow Steinbeck was known to use.

## First Writing Endeavors

It was during his senior year at Mississippi State University that Grisham began a novel about small-town southern residents. Although he gave up on the book, some of the elements of that early work did emerge again in his first published book, *A Time to Kill*. Today Grisham seems almost embarrassed by his initial effort at writing:

> I don't want to say what the plot was, because it was so bad. I tried to do it fast while taking some difficult accounting courses. Basically, it dealt with local characters in small-town Mississippi. I've always wanted to write about people like this because the list of story ideas is absolutely limitless.[9]

Once Grisham completed those "difficult accounting courses," he graduated from Mississippi State University in 1977 with a bachelor of science degree in accounting. He had previously been accepted to the law school at the University of Mississippi; with his diploma from Mississippi State in hand, he moved to Oxford, Mississippi, to study tax law. It was not long, however, until Grisham once again felt a sense of dissatisfaction. He found tax law boring and decided to switch to criminal law.

Finally settled into a specialty of the legal profession he found more interesting, Grisham stuck with law school, but he did not give up writing. Eventually he developed a desire to become a published author and began studying the writing business even while still studying law:

> Throughout my school years, I read constantly and became familiar with what books were getting published. As a result, I came to believe that my story idea could also be published. No one knew I was attempting a second book and my plan was to finish it before I married and completed law school. But lord, it took a month just to write, type, and revise the first chapter.[10]

The plot of Grisham's second attempted novel dealt with an international terrorist incident; however, after giving up on the book later in the year, he never went back to that particular story line. Grisham realized there was no way he could finish writing a novel before he finished law school. He turned his attention back to his studies.

People who knew Grisham in those days had no idea he was a novice writer. One of his law professors, Guthrie Abbott, recalls that Grisham gave no clues about his passion for writing: "I remember him well. He was a good student and did real well in my class. But I would not have said he was going to write the great American novel, or the great American movie."[11]

John Grisham graduated from the University of Mississippi in 1981. Later that same year he passed the bar exam, a test all law school graduates must pass to become licensed attorneys.

Also during this period Grisham married Renee Jones in the First Baptist Church of Oxford. Jones and Grisham had known each other from their high school years in their hometown of

*As a lawyer Grisham became disgusted with each criminal and civil case he represented, eventually leading him to return to his writing.*

Southaven. Grisham refers to his wife as "the little girl next door who grew up while I wasn't looking." [12]

## Young Attorney and Politician

After the wedding the young couple returned to Southaven, where Grisham opened a law office. His first case involved a man who was claiming self-defense after shooting his wife's lover in the head. Although Grisham won the case, he earned a mere one thousand dollars. This slight financial gain caused a disgust that would slowly grow with each criminal and civil case he represented. Despite the fact he won many trials and lawsuits, Grisham grew weary of the whole profession. He returned to his writing, which he had set aside in law school, and realized he loved writing more than he loved winning in court. "I found myself . . . representing people I didn't really like in cases that were boring," he recalls. "Once I started writing the first book, the law couldn't measure up." [13]

At about the same time that Grisham became disillusioned with practicing law and started writing his next novel, he also decided to run for the Mississippi House of Representatives. His motivation to seek public office was based on his desire to make the state's education system more focused on children's needs. His campaign for the state legislature also coincided with the birth of his first child. Scott Ross, John Grisham's friend and roommate while the legislature was in session, comments on Grisham's decision to seek public office:

> John ran for office when Mississippi was rallying to dilute the power of the current speaker of the house. This long standing politician didn't support a kindergarten program and it upset many voters.[14]

In November 1983 voters of the Seventh District elected Democrat John Grisham as their state representative. In early 1984 Grisham headed to Jackson, the state capital, to begin his first term. He wasted no time in supporting education reform and threw his political muscle behind "Mississippi's BEST" (Better Education for Success Tomorrow) legislation. Mississippi's BEST was a broad-based legislative package of goals and programs to offer children in Mississippi a chance for a world-class education by the year 2001.

During his two terms as a state representative, Grisham dedicated his time and talent to many other issues besides education. A few of these issues have been featured in the plot lines of his novels, including the controversy over punitive damage legislation. Grisham was against this particular legislation, also referred to as tort reform, because it would limit the dollar amount of the awards given to winners of lawsuits against insurance companies. Punitive damages are the monetary compensations awarded to a plaintiff in a lawsuit to punish a guilty defendant of gross negligence. These types of damages showed up as a secondary plot point in Grisham's book *The Rainmaker*.

In *The Rainmaker,* young lawyer Rudy Baylor makes a negative reference to tort reform while representing a mother whose son is being denied medical coverage from an insurance company. In the novel, Baylor wins his case and the insurance company is slapped with punitive damages totaling millions of dollars.

*Many of the issues that Grisham feels strongly about show up in his novels.* The Rainmaker, *for example, is about the controversy over punitive damage legislation.*

In February 1987 Grisham wrote a letter responding to a supporter of tort reform who had asked him to consider the merits of the legislation. Grisham's letter not only blasts the entire tort reform premise, but it also reflects his no-nonsense writing style and honesty that are so popular among readers.

Dear Mr. Greene:

Last week I received your letter regarding tort reform. . . .

It is difficult for me to understand how an intelligent and successful man like yourself can be so misled and brainwashed by the propaganda spewing forth from the insurance industry.

In the next paragraphs Grisham includes statistics to support his position and then closes with an even livelier choice of words.

Do you honestly believe that your friends, employees, relatives, and colleagues, as jurors, are so stupid and gullible to return million dollar awards for plaintiffs who don't deserve them?

Come on, Mr. Greene. Open your eyes. . . . If I honestly believed that tort reform would help the liability insurance crisis, then I would seriously consider some of these measures. But in reality, tort reform is the biggest lie now being told to you and the American public.[15]

Before his second term was over, Grisham had dealt with the reapportionment of districts, highway projects, and even salaries and staff concerns of state government attorneys. He also served on several legislative committees, including the Judiciary A and Military Affairs Committees.

Scott Ross suggests that Grisham's legislative record sparked rumors of a possible U.S. Senate race at the end of his term as state representative. The Democrats were desperate to find a strong candidate to oppose Republican Trent Lott. Grisham jokingly dismissed the idea, referring to his affinity for going without socks or a fresh shave. In the May 19, 1993, issue of the *Clarion-Ledger*, a political cartoon shows a fellow Democrat pleading with Grisham to run for the Senate. Grisham, holding a little-league bat, replies, "Not in a month of Sundays. Go find yourself another stooge to knock off Lott."

In spite of his accomplishments during his tenure in the Mississippi House of Representatives, Grisham often felt restless and bored in the state capital. He also missed his family, which now included a son, Ty, and a daughter, Shea. With Southaven located in the northwest corner of the state and Jackson almost in the center of the state, Grisham did a lot of traveling to spend as much time as possible with his family. Scott Ross admired his friend's sense of priorities:

He did not let the legislature interfere with his family. He was especially committed to his wife and children and they came first. John was one of the few people in the legislature who knew what was permanent and what was temporary.[16]

By the time his second term ended, Grisham could feel career dissatisfaction tugging at him once more. He was tired of the frequent inactivity of the legislature, and although he was still practicing law, his real joy came from writing. He had written three books in the years he had been working as a lawyer and serving in the Mississippi legislature, and one of these books had already been sold to a filmmaker in Hollywood. Even so, Grisham would never leave law completely. After all, he loved writing down his ideas, which were based on cases he had worked on or heard about in the small towns of the Deep South.

# Chapter 3

# An Inspired Writer

During the process of writing his first published novel, John Grisham learned something that every successful writer learns: Writers have to be passionate about their topics, disciplined in their work habits, enthusiastic about selling their work to publishers, and dedicated to their careers as professional writers.

## The Passion to Write

Grisham's idea for *A Time to Kill* came to him after walking into a courtroom one day in De Soto County, Mississippi. He was awestruck by the testimony of a young female witness who had been brutally raped and left for dead. "I never felt such emotion and human drama in my life," Grisham later recalled. "I wondered what it would be like if the girl's father killed the rapist and was put on trial. I had to write it down." [17] And so he did write it down, every spare chance he got, for the next three years. When asked later on what he found so satisfying about writing, Grisham replied:

> When I started all this, my motives were pure, I was not driven by greed or money. I had a story. It was a courtroom drama. I was doing a lot of courtroom work . . . handling a lot of court appointed criminal cases, in trial law . . . . And I kept telling myself, I would like to be the lawyer who defended a father who murdered the two guys who raped his daughter. One thing led to another, and I was sort of consumed by the story. [18]

## The Discipline to Write

Grisham demonstrated his disciplined work habits through the routine he established of writing from 5:00 until 7:00 each morning. At

7:00 he would stop so he could prepare for his court appear-
ances that day. Grisham admits that the schedule was hard on
him, and at times he felt exhausted:

> I'd get up and go to the office that early. . . . And I re-
> member several times being in court at nine o'clock in
> the morning, really tired, because writing takes a lot out
> of you. It's draining. And I would do it for an hour or
> two in the morning, and get ready for court, and go to
> court. Be standing, waiting for the judge, and be really
> tired.[19]

For the three years he worked on *A Time to Kill*, Grisham
wrote as often as possible, not only in the mornings but also during breaks in court and between consultations with clients in his
law office. He even wrote while waiting for sessions to begin in
the state legislature. Grisham put every bit of creative energy toward that book, and even now, with a decade full of best-sellers
behind him, he still has a soft spot in his heart for his first proj-
ect. The book also demonstrates his passion for writing about
southern towns and their unique people:

> *A Time to Kill* was a special book to me. It was my first
> one. I poured my guts into it for three years and it was
> so dear. I love the book because it was set in the
> south. . . . Those are the ones I like to read and the ones
> I like to write.[20]

The completed novel was originally titled *Deathnell*. However, a manuscript page on display in the John Grisham Room
at the Mississippi State University (MSU) library has that title
crossed out and *A Time to Kill* written in ink above it.
    The John Grisham Room, located in the Mitchell Memorial
Library on the MSU campus, is a tribute to Grisham's work.
Among the displays are several yellow legal pads on which
Grisham wrote the first draft of *A Time to Kill*. Eventually he
transcribed all the handwritten work so he could submit the material to agents and publishers. Next to the yellow pads and original typed manuscript is an article that states that his early typing

## The John Grisham Room at MSU

In a brochure provided for visitors, Mississippi State University's Mitchell Memorial Library acknowledges the generosity of John Grisham. The John Grisham Room contains various items that Grisham has donated, such as original pages from manuscripts that were handwritten by the author on yellow legal pads.

During dedication ceremonies for Mississippi State's John Grisham Room, the novelist and university alumnus told those gathered that he wanted the room put to use. He said, "My biggest hope is that it will inspire students to read, perhaps to write, and, most importantly, to dream."

The John Grisham Room is located in the university's state-of-the-art Mitchell Memorial Library, which recently underwent a $15 million renovation and expansion. The collection is uniquely situated to offer opportunities to fulfill Mr. Grisham's vision—opportunities for those who visit to be inspired to read, write, and dream.

*The John Grisham Room at Mississippi State University.*

*John Grisham (second from right) at the dedication of the John Grisham Room.*

was done on a word processor set up between the washer and dryer in his utility room.

Not only do the items in the John Grisham Room offer inspiration to would-be writers, they also offer clues about Grisham's writing processes. The typed manuscript pages contain handwritten comments from trusted colleagues who read Grisham's work before it hit the store shelves. Many of these notations were made by his wife, Renee. She is one of his most influential readers, critiquing his finished product and encouraging him to follow up on some ideas and disregard others.

Grisham's friend and fellow writer T. R. Pearson indicates that Renee is a key partner in the writing process of every Grisham novel:

> Renee serves as Grisham's sounding board and least sympathetic reader. She subjects each novel to what she refers to as the assault. . . . Once an idea has passed muster and Grisham has begun to turn it into a novel, Renee reads it in 100-page batches. She offers advice and encouragement as a rule, but on occasion the flutter and thump of an

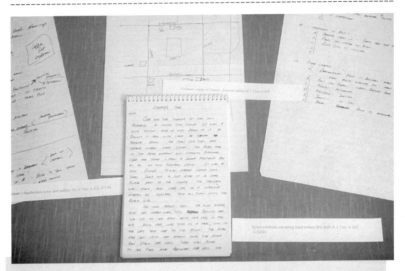

*The John Grisham Room contains hand-written pages from manuscripts that Grisham himself has donated.*

offending installment being flung across the room can be heard. By the time the book is published, Renee has more than earned a place on the dedication page.[21]

Grisham agrees that Renee's role is crucial to the success of his writing. In one interview he said Renee's influence helps him see and fix potential problems with his ideas and writing:

> I constantly inundate Renee with all sorts of story ideas, and it's her job to tell me to shut up and keep searching. She has an uncanny ability to spot a good story; I tend to think that almost anything will work. Once I start writing, she is merciless as the chapters pour forth. She enjoys picking a good brawl over a subplot, a weak character, an unnecessary scene. I accuse her of looking for trouble—and inevitably, I return to the typewriter and fix whatever troubles her.[22]

As much as Grisham relies on his wife's intellect and keen sense of story, Renee is not the only one who offers suggestions and an objective eye to his works in progress. Marc Smirnoff, editor of the regional Mississippi magazine *Oxford American,* edits Grisham's books and sends along detailed lists of notes.

David Gernert, who was once Grisham's editor at Doubleday, now serves as his agent. Gernert is still a major influence when it comes to cutting unnecessary words while making sure all necessary plot information is in a novel.

Grisham has learned that revision is a vital part of the writing process. When he finished *A Time to Kill*, it was nearly a year before he sold the novel to Wynwood Press. He then discovered that revision is a task every writer faces after selling something to a publisher. Grisham considered the revision chore as simply an editor and writer working together to improve a book. He was not upset about being asked to rewrite a few things, and he was even proud of the job he did:

> While they wanted some things cut, they also wanted some embellishment, particularly in strengthening some of the characters. Dealing with editors is much like negotiating across a table between two opposing sides. The difference is that the writer and editor are working toward the same goal—to make the book as good as it can be. Eighty percent of the book is my original manuscript and I wrote all the revisions.[23]

## The Enthusiasm to Sell

Grisham sold *A Time to Kill* to Wynwood with the help of his agent at the time, Jay Garon. Finding an agent, however, was no easy task. The process began with a carefully planned strategy and a large amount of patience:

> I sat down with my secretary and we made up two lists. One contained the names and addresses of 30 publishing house editors; the other, 30 names and addresses of literary agents. Having already put together a package containing a query letter, book summary, and first three chapters, I had the secretary make 10 copies of each. She was to send a copy of each to the first five editors on the first list and the same to the first agents on the second.[24]

When one package came back rejected, he simply had his secretary bundle the materials again and send it off to the next

*Grisham credits his wife,
Renee, for her role in the
success of his writing. Her
suggestions are often used in
revisions, which took a year
to do for* A Time to Kill.

name on the list. Grisham was willing to stick with his plan for as long as it took to get what he wanted. "I never thought of quitting," he says. "My attitude was, 'What the heck, let's have some fun.' I honestly believe I would've sent it to several hundred people before I would have even thought of giving up."[25]

After several weeks three agents replied, each saying they wanted to represent him to publishers. Obtaining Garon to represent him was a major accomplishment for a first-time novelist, especially since Garon said he is careful about who he represents:

I'm not a philanthropic institution, I have a payroll to meet each week. So I try to be selective in the materials and clients I handle. But with John's first book, I spotted his unique talent.[26]

Once Jay Garon was working for him, it was still another year before Wynwood Press made an offer to purchase the book. During that time Grisham barraged Garon with phone calls, wanting to know how the selling aspect was going. His agent encouraged him to concentrate on writing the second book to take his mind off selling the first one. Grisham did as he was told and finished working on *The Firm*. When he sent the outline to Garon, the agent was thrilled:

> When he sent me the first draft, I read it totally. I started reading at 10 o'clock at night and I didn't go to sleep because I couldn't put it down. It's what you call compulsive reading.[27]

Garon's comment about not being able to stop reading once he started is common among readers of Grisham's books. Grisham believes his easy, right-to-the-point style is what fans appreciate in his books: "I have had readers say they liked the book [*A Time to Kill*] because it 'really flowed.' When I began, I simply sat down and began with the rape and ended with the

## Dave Barry on John Grisham

Many of John Grisham's readers use his legal thrillers to keep themselves amused during otherwise boring airplane flights. In his syndicated column for June 21, 1993, humorist Dave Barry saluted his fellow writer.

> Like most people, I can always use an extra $7 or $8 million, which is why today I have decided to write a blockbuster legal thriller.

> Americans buy legal thrillers by the ton. I was in many airports over the past few months, and I got the impression that aviation authorities were making this announcement over the public-address system: "FEDERAL REGULATIONS PROHIBIT YOU FROM BOARDING A PLANE UNLESS YOU ARE CARRYING 'THE CLIENT' BY JOHN GRISHAM." I mean, EVERYBODY had this book. ("This is the captain speaking. We'll be landing in Seattle instead of Detroit because I want to finish 'The Client.'")

verdict. I wanted it to move quickly. I can't write any other way. I have no patience with writers . . . who try to be obtuse and obscure. When I read, I want a good story, well-told." [28]

Wynwood printed five thousand copies of *A Time to Kill* and Grisham bought one thousand of those himself. He then visited bookstores throughout Arkansas and Mississippi, building long-time relationships with bookstore owners and readers. His marketing efforts helped his first book to sell well—a book that many people only considered a regional novel that would appeal mostly to readers in the Deep South.

In his second published novel, Grisham retained his straightforward style and applied it to a broader topic—the Mafia, murder, and greed.

In *The Firm,* the main character is Mitch McDeere, a recent Harvard law graduate who is looking for a big law firm that will pay him a huge salary. He is in debt and needs the money and security a large firm can provide. What he finds is a law firm backed by an infamous Chicago crime family. Before long Mitch realizes that his future consists of three options: being jailed for performing illegal acts for the firm, providing evidence to the FBI about the firm and then living on the run from the Mafia, or ending up dead—as had happened to two other members who betrayed the firm.

Despite Garon's enthusiasm for *The Firm,* he had trouble selling the book to publishers. Still, Garon believed in the writer and the book's content and knew the novel would make a great film. He recruited an associate in Hollywood to peddle the film rights.

When the film company Paramount bought the rights for six hundred thousand dollars, Garon suddenly had no trouble grabbing the attention of New York publishers who wanted to take advantage of the publicity a hit movie could provide. Grisham recalls that early fever when Paramount bought the screen rights to *The Firm,* and Garon could then sell the novel to a publisher: "The day that news came out in the *New York Times,* my agent had 18 calls from publishers. He had a lot of fun negotiating that deal." [29]

Later, when the sales figures came in and the book inched its way up the best-seller list, Grisham had trouble believing how popular his second novel had become. "It was a tremendous

*Although his second novel retained the straightforward style that Grisham is known for,* The Firm *contained broader topics such as the Mafia, murder, and greed.*

surprise," he recalls. "I didn't know what to expect, but it surely wasn't this." [30]

John Grisham's life changed once more in a dramatic manner that day. He now knew that he wanted to spend his time writing rather than practicing law. He also realized that *The Firm* was being more widely received than *A Time to Kill.* If he wanted to continue writing novels for a living rather than as a therapeutic hobby, he would have to wrestle with story decisions in the future.

## Dedication to Career

Grisham had to make a choice about the content of his next novel. Would he write a plot-driven book, which increased the reader's desire to keep turning pages, or a social-issue book, which focused more on character development and slowed the pace?

Although he loved *A Time to Kill,* a social-issue book dealing with racism, *The Firm,* with its plot twists and turns, was more marketable. Realizing this, Grisham has tended to use fast-paced

*With its plot twists and turns,* The Firm *was criticized as a fast-paced novel lacking in character development.*

plots in his novels. This choice won him good reviews early in his career, as Frederic Koeppel points out in his 1991 article in the newspaper the *Commercial Appeal,* shortly after *The Firm* hit the best-seller list: "*The Firm* received generally favorable notices and was reviewed in enviable circles: *Newsweek, Cosmopolitan, People* and other national magazines and newspapers."[31]

Some literary critics, however, derided Grisham's decision to write a fast-paced story in a short amount of time. Most negative comments about his early novels center on the lack of character development, which many writers accomplish through devices such as telling readers of a character's inner thoughts and motivations as they relate to the plot. For example, in *John Grisham: A Critical Companion,* author Mary Beth Pringle writes:

> Characters in *The Firm* are not fully developed; that is, readers know them more as types than as real human beings. . . . We don't, however, know much about the inner workings of Mitch's mind: what he thinks and dreams about.

Although Mitch is underdeveloped, he shares obvious qualities with Jake Brigance in Grisham's first novel, *A Time to Kill*.[32]

As the author of the only book analyzing the literary quality of John Grisham's works, Pringle has paid more attention to his novels than some other reviewers, who were even more critical. Marilyn Stasio, a reviewer for the *New York Times*, had this to say about Grisham's plot-driven novels: "They say that he forces you to keep on flipping pages, but then so does a Rolodex."[33]

Grisham has said that he has tried to learn from the more reasonable comments regarding his early works. His later books show improvement, although his third published novel, *The Pelican Brief*—which he wrote in a record one hundred days—was once again criticized for lack of character development. In her comments about *The Pelican Brief*'s main character, Pringle states:

> Darby Shaw, Grisham's protagonist in *The Pelican Brief*, is the case in point. Although she changes disguises frequently and cuts her hair shorter and shorter, she is the same perky law student at the end of *The Pelican Brief*

*A story about a legal brief regarding the assassinations of Supreme Court justices—*The Pelican Brief—*was written in a record one hundred days.*

## John Grisham and Book Reviews

Every writer must learn to deal with criticism. As popular as Grisham is among his readers, he says he has suffered his share of bad reviews.

*The only place where* A Time to Kill *got reviewed was the Memphis paper—my home paper—and they trashed it. That was a deep wound that has never healed. Then* The Firm *came out, and most reviews were pretty good.* Pelican Brief *was painful from coast to coast. I'd read a bad review and want to go out and kill people.* The Client *was next and it got trashed—the reviews started talking about the fame and the money. Pat Conroy (*The Prince of Tides*) told me, "Your life is a whole lot easier if you stop reading reviews." So I stopped reading almost all of them.*

—Interview with Mark Harris, "Attorney's Privileges,"
*Entertainment Weekly,* May 5, 1995.

that she was in the beginning. . . . It does not show or comment on how being on the run affects her nor how it "challenged" her to be anything other than what she was originally.[34]

Other critics have called Grisham's works repetitive, citing that they often feature a lawyer or law student fighting an obstacle bigger than themselves. Then again, those are essential elements in a legal thriller. *The Pelican Brief,* for example, features law student Darby Shaw, who composes a legal brief, a written legal opinion, regarding recent assassinations of Supreme Court justices. When the wrong person reads her brief, Darby realizes that she has to run to stay one step ahead of the killer.

*The Pelican Brief* was also made into a feature-length film in 1993, and Grisham seemed pleased by the novel's success: "*The Pelican Brief* delivered. It satisfied a lot of readers. It was a critical book for me."[35]

This third novel was published shortly after Grisham resigned from the Mississippi House of Representatives, closed his law practice in Southaven, and moved to Oxford. Whatever his feelings about the book's success, he could now focus solely on writing. He knew writing would provide a healthy financial future for his family, and he went to work as a full-time writer.

# Chapter 4

# A Publishing Phenomenon

Oₙᴄᴇ ʜᴇ ᴀɴᴅ his family were established in Oxford, Grisham turned his attention to both professional and personal goals, which included producing one book a year and building a baseball field for the local Little League teams to use. While accomplishing both goals, he soon discovered that he would have to deal with other, less positive, aspects of being a celebrity.

Grisham found that preserving any sense of privacy was becoming increasingly difficult. Other negative aspects in his new career were derogatory remarks about the quality of his writing and his frustrating encounters with film producers in Hollywood. He also faced the nasty task of filing a lawsuit against Jay Garon's literary agency.

To overcome these distractions, Grisham focused both on protecting his family from unwanted publicity as well as on his right to create the plot-driven novels that he felt his readers wanted. To accomplish the second goal he spent as much time as possible writing, only leaving his house to attend PTA meetings and to coach Little League baseball.

Grisham would most likely agree that the baseball field he built next to his Oxford home is one of the things that kept him grounded and calm during his early years as a best-selling author. In a 1993 interview marking the release of his fourth book, *The Client*, Grisham said, "That's my calling in life, to coach Little League baseball."[36]

During a tour of the baseball field he had built for his son's team to practice on, he told the interviewer that he needed to

*To overcome distractions of unwanted publicity, Grisham built a baseball field for his son's team to practice on.*

move the fence—the kids had gotten so big that they were hitting homers right and left. Even as *The Client* was landing in the bookstores, Grisham could not keep his mind off baseball.

## *The Client*—Another Success

The success of his fourth book allowed Grisham to relax a little, and reviews for *The Client* were much more positive than the comments regarding his previous novels. With *The Client*, Grisham had taken to heart some of the comments from earlier reviews and spent more time developing his main characters.

Mary Beth Pringle, whose comments on his first three books repeatedly pointed out poor characterization, also points out his successful attempt with *The Client*:

> Grisham must take seriously the reviews of his work, because he seems to have worked hard to develop his protagonist heroes in *The Client* (Mark Sway and Reggie

Love) more fully than his protagonists in earlier novels. Readers of fiction expect characters who seem real . . . who feel the same emotions they would feel. Mark Sway is that kind of character, one whose actions *and* thoughts readers are allowed to share.[37]

## Building Character

Character development is the way *The Client* differs from Grisham's first three novels. Readers learn Mark and Reggie's inner thoughts, fears, and worries throughout the book. Mark changes and grows during the action that takes place, and readers are a part of his decisions as well as Reggie's thoughts and feelings.

The book is fast-paced, with plenty of suspenseful moments; yet Grisham still is able to weave in greater character insight. *The Client* sold well, too: A report in *Forbes* magazine listed Grisham's income for 1992–1993 at $25 million.

The combination of a fast-paced plot and strong characterization worked well for his fifth book as well. In *The Chamber*, Grisham took a controversial social issue and built the reader's interest by creating more complex characters.

*The Chamber* focused on the issue of the death penalty and how the characters interacted with each other. Grisham knew that characterization would be even more difficult since he chose to open the novel with a scene that leaves the reader feeling no sympathy for the person facing execution.

When asked his thoughts about *The Chamber*, Grisham acknowledged that his novel had less action; he also expressed hope that it would broaden his audience: "It's much more about the people. It will appeal to many different kinds of readers."[38]

The sales figures for *The Chamber* suggest that Grisham was right not to doubt his book's potential. The publisher, Doubleday, printed 2.5 million copies, basing the figure on *The Client*'s sales, which were just under 3 million.

Readers of *The Chamber* found a slower pace and a more subtle tension than in Grisham's other books. Sam Cayhall, the condemned criminal, is certainly guilty of murder, and his new lawyer, Adam Hall, is the grandson he had never met. In their

*Taking to heart some of the earlier criticisms, Grisham paid close attention to developing the main characters of* The Client.

first stormy meeting, it is clear that they do not see eye to eye on anything. The suspense builds as these characters learn more about one another and ultimately begin to care for each other as the deadline for Cayhall's execution approaches.

Reviewers gave the book positive ratings. As one critic wrote, "All the elements that have made Grisham a successful (and rich) writer are here: fine writing, believable characters, social comment, courtroom drama, and legal maneuvers a layman can figure out." [39]

*The Chamber* was so successful that the publisher had trouble keeping books in its own office building. Grisham was impressed when he strolled through Doubleday's eighteenth-floor reception area one day and noticed a large display promoting *The Chamber.* However, his pride turned to curiosity when he saw only empty book jackets in the display. Ellen Archer, director of publicity for Doubleday, told him, "People keep stealing the books!" [40]

## A Popular Writer

The intense drama that temporarily turned employees of a publishing firm into petty thieves also won Grisham millions of fans. Most people would classify Grisham's writing as excellent popular fiction—and that is fine with him: He never intended to write great literature. Grisham wanted people to enjoy his books, and they have. In an interview shortly after his sixth book, *The Rainmaker*, was published, Grisham offered more detail concerning his philosophy of writing:

> People have come to expect my books to provide a certain amount of entertainment. . . . I think I've always realized where my talents are. I'm not a great stylist, but I can come up with a good plot. And that's what I try to do.[41]

Grisham believes that his dedication to entertainment is what makes his legal thrillers more popular and more successful than books of the same category written by others. In one interview

*The success of* The Chamber, *a story about the death penalty, was so great that the publisher had trouble keeping the books in its own office building.*

Grisham stated that he believes that some legal-fiction writers fail to insert enough tension in their stories:

> There are a lot of lawyers writing books, but most of them are not very good. They tend to deal too much with the mechanics of trials, stuff that tends to be kind of flat. The biggest mistake lawyers make in writing books is not keeping up enough suspense.[42]

Other observers suggest that Grisham's success lies in the fact that his writing is well-rounded. Richard Howarth, owner of Square Books in Oxford, uses the word *satisfying* to describe Grisham's appeal:

> Some people attribute his sales to hype, but actually the books are well-written, suspenseful, and satisfying in a way that a lot of books aren't. There are books that are more literary, there are books that have more complex plots, and there are books that have more fully conceived characters, but when you take everything and put it all together, there's no one out there who is writing books that have such a combination of all those elements.[43]

These elements have certainly earned Grisham the superstar status reached only by a handful of other writers, including Stephen King and Michael Crichton.

For Grisham, a downside to this popularity was a lack of privacy. Tour buses had been stopping regularly at the driveway to his Oxford home, but he lost all patience when a young couple showed up to exchange their wedding vows on his front lawn.

As much as Grisham loved the Victorian home he had built on his sixty-seven-acre ranch, he scouted out a new location where he and his family could enjoy their privacy. After finding a suitable hideaway outside of Charlottesville, Virginia, he shared some of his thoughts with his friends and readers of the *Clarion-Ledger:*

> If privacy is something you value and you start losing it, you take drastic measures. Leaving Oxford was a drastic measure because we never thought we'd leave. We were

happy there. The kids were happy with their friends and school. Leaving wasn't easy. I miss my home in Oxford every day. And we come back every chance we get. . . . My office is in Oxford. My secretary is in Oxford. The staff that worked at our house and farm are still working there. . . . We've had a wonderful time in Virginia, but I still don't think the move is permanent. But then I'm not sure what permanent is.[44]

In his sixth book, *The Rainmaker,* readers learn even more about Grisham's personality. Grisham says that in this novel it is basically his smart mouth the reader hears through the first-person narration of Rudy Baylor.

This statement suggests that Baylor's character reflects a great deal of Grisham's thought processes and feelings. It also clues his audiences into the passion behind his more recent novels and the issues they tackle. Grisham's protagonist in *The Rainmaker* is a fresh law student who is fighting the evils of a monster health insurance company.

*The main character in* The Rainmaker *reflects Grisham's own personality—a young law student going up against a giant health insurance company.*

Grisham is not shy about admitting that his sixth novel is based partly on fact:

> The story started because of a real trial (held years ago) in rural Mississippi. . . . There were just too many stories about it, I don't know what's fact or fiction, but it's still talked about in legal circles in Mississippi.[45]

In *The Rainmaker*, Grisham treats the reader to a situation similar to those in his early novels: a young attorney facing giants. Yet, the character development is much more pronounced, so the suspense comes from how the events will change and affect the people in the story.

In *The Runaway Jury*, however, Grisham's seventh book, his intentional omission of detailed characterization of jury members is necessary to the story's ending. The reader is kept guessing about a mysterious juror, Nicholas Easter, and his helper, Marlee.

With his popularity so high, Grisham enjoyed the luxury of being able to educate people about the darker side of big business and the legal profession. Both *The Rainmaker* and *The Runaway Jury* deal with social issues that Grisham was interested in bringing to the public's attention. Through his fiction Grisham could highlight what he saw as the dangers of tort reform and the problem of jury tampering.

## Hollywood Hype and Scandal

The popularity of Grisham's works naturally attracted the attention of moviemakers. Selling movie rights to his novels has sent Grisham's income into the millions of dollars. He is certainly aware of the opportunities Hollywood provides for successful authors. For example, Grisham agreed to write an original screenplay—one not based on any of his previous books. What appeared to be an opportunity could, he learned, have an unfortunate outcome.

One such disaster was *The Gingerbread Man*, the film for which he wrote the screenplay. It starred such big name actors as Kenneth Branagh, Robert Duvall, and Daryl Hannah, yet

*Grisham was so outraged that his screenplay for* The Gingerbread Man *had been reworked and that so much vulgarity had been added that he demanded his name be taken off the credits.*

Grisham was outraged with the result. The director, Robert Altman, had reworked the script and added so much vulgarity that Grisham demanded his name taken off the credits as a writer. Today the film simply states that the movie is based on a story by John Grisham.

Grisham understands both the benefits and risks each film-associated sale offers. When he was interviewed during a visit to Los Angeles, Grisham gave these insights:

> I've always had the attitude with movies that I get as much money up front as I can, I kiss it good-bye and I expect it to be different. And if I don't like it I don't have to sell film rights.[46]

Unlike *The Gingerbread Man*, films made from other Grisham novels have stayed relatively true to the original works, and for the most part, Grisham has been pleased with the results. When *A Time to Kill* was being made into a movie, Grisham spent a great deal of time on location with the film crew and coached the young lead actor, Matthew McConaughey, about what to do and not do in a courtroom.

*Although valuing his privacy, Grisham has found that Hollywood has certainly expanded his readership.*

Grisham's dealings with Hollywood also led him to become involved in a lawsuit against Jay Garon's literary agency shortly after Garon died. Grisham claimed that he was not told about certain fees collected from movie producers, which were then sent to Garon's lawyer, Elliot J. Lefkowitz. Grisham asked for damages and a termination of his contract with the agency.

The agency claimed that Grisham was simply trying to get out of his contract because Garon had passed away; Grisham maintained that his motivation had nothing to do with wanting to leave the agency but everything to do with getting money that was rightfully his. Grisham's attorney, Michael Rudell, commenting on the case, emphasized his client's character, saying the defendant's claim of betrayal was weak and not at all justified. Rudell cited the fact that Grisham was not told about the payments for the lawsuit. "Grisham is an extremely loyal, honorable, giving person," Rudell asserted. "The payments most definitely were not disclosed to him, and that is really the source of his outrage about this."[47]

In spite of the unpleasantness of the lawsuit against Garon's agency and the frustration over story-line changes in his films, Grisham's relationship with Hollywood has certainly helped expand his readership. Yet, even with the benefits of successful film dealings, he has never abandoned his personal priorities in favor of Hollywood glamour. He still values his privacy, his family, and his loyal readers as much as he did when he autographed the first few copies of *A Time to Kill*.

# Chapter 5

----------------------------------------

# Back to the Basics

JOHN GRISHAM HOPED more than anything to remain unchanged by the celebrity status his writing has brought him. He has managed to accomplish that goal to a remarkable extent. For example, loyalty to friends is a value he has retained, even as changes in his professional life force him to adapt.

## A New Partner

The death of his original agent, Jay Garon, and the disagreement with the company Garon left behind, forced Grisham to hire a new agent. In this decision his loyal nature guided his choice. Grisham invited David Gernert, his editor at Doubleday, to leave the publishing house and start a literary agency with Grisham as his premier author.

Grisham's proposal was an affirmation of trust in Gernert and a lucrative offer to the editor. Most agents are rewarded 10 to 15 percent of whatever their authors earn from their work. Thus, each time Grisham sold a book to a publisher, the book's film rights, foreign rights, or audio rights, Gernert would earn more with each sale than he ever made with Doubleday.

Grisham trusts his new agent's judgment completely. Perhaps that confidence stems from the fact that Gernert has edited all of Grisham's novels with Doubleday and will continue to do so. No doubt Grisham recognizes a pattern of success that he and Gernert have already established. The fact that Grisham and Gernert are great friends has made this a partnership that each man can enjoy and from which each can benefit.

Gernert also plays the role of Grisham's protector, referring to his agency as a type of clearinghouse for whoever would like a piece of his star client:

> A fairly large part of what we do is handle the requests that come in for John to do—everything from give a keynote speech, to appear in a commercial, to write an essay for *Newsweek,* or whatever.[48]

Gernert and other advisers wonder if Grisham's immense popularity could cause a Grisham overload. Each book's sales seem to cap off just below Doubleday's standard print run of 2.8 million. Grisham has also worried about overexposure caused by so many of his works surfacing simultaneously. In his slow, soft southern drawl he recently explained:

> Well, we've been worried about overexposure for a long time. There was a time about three or four years ago when *The Chamber* was number one in hardback and *The Firm, The Pelican Brief,* and *A Time to Kill,* or something like that, were one, two, and three in paper. And there was a movie out, I think it was *The Client.* That was about as crazy as everything could possibly get. We talked a lot about overexposure and worried a lot about it, and still do.[49]

Some people in the publishing industry believe this inundation of Grisham products may have caused him to hesitate about selling film rights to his books *The Partner* and *The Street Lawyer.* Grisham's response is to say that Hollywood offers an additional stress that he does not always want to endure. This statement came on the heels of a controversy involving Grisham and one of Hollywood's best-known movie directors.

## Taking a Stand

In 1996, shortly after the release of *The Runaway Jury,* Grisham found himself embroiled in an issue that had been building in the entertainment industry for years: the increasing violence portrayed in films. This controversy, which had nothing to do with any of the movies based on Grisham's books, focused on a movie Oliver Stone directed titled *Natural Born Killers.* When it opened in theaters, the level of violence was appalling to many movie patrons.

*Grisham became concerned with the increasing portrayal of violence in such movies as* Natural Born Killers.

When the movie hit video stores, it became a hot rental and drew strong criticism again after a young couple supposedly watched the movie repeatedly and headed off on a killing spree similar to the one depicted in the film.

An old acquaintance of Grisham's, William Savage from Mississippi, was one of the couple's victims. Grisham stood up as a supporter of the grieving family and denounced Stone's work. Grisham's argument first appeared in the *Oxford American*, and excerpts were later reprinted in *Vanity Fair* magazine. Grisham accused the movie of being a disturbing piece of commercial sensationalism made only for its shock value:

> Oliver Stone has said that *Natural Born Killers* was meant to be a satire on our culture's appetite for violence and the media's craving for it. . . . It is a relentlessly bloody story designed to shock us and to numb us further to the senselessness of reckless murder.[50]

Grisham then stated his belief that a filmmaker should be held accountable for damages done by his product:

> Think of a film as a product, something created and brought to market. . . . Though the law has yet to declare movies to be products, it is only one small step away. If

something goes wrong with the product, whether by design or defect, and injury ensues, then its makers are held responsible.[51]

These were strong statements, especially from a man who prefers to avoid publicity. There was also a touch of irony in Grisham's call for legislation that would hold creators of a film accountable for a movie's influence if it caused personal injury. After all, Grisham himself had been known for, and made a great deal of money from, movies with violent scenes. Oliver Stone pounced on this fact in his rebuttal to Grisham's comments:

> The fact is, Mr. Grisham has become a very rich man off a body of work which utilizes violent crime as a foundation for mass entertainment.

> For example, his book, *A Time to Kill,* has as its protagonist a man who murders with clear premeditation two young racists who raped his 10-year-old daughter (a rape which Mr. Grisham writes about in horrifyingly graphic detail). The man's lawyer wins his freedom for these murders of vengeance.[52]

*Oliver Stone was criticized by Grisham for creating a movie that was designed to "numb us further to the senselessness of reckless murder."*

By pointing out Grisham's use of detailed crime scenes, Stone makes an interesting point. He went on to say that if lawmakers took to heart Grisham's argument of liability, then Grisham himself should be held accountable for any revenge murder if that criminal has ever watched *A Time to Kill*. Although censorship of movie content is still being debated, Grisham's position helped draw attention to accountability among moviemakers.

## Moral Issues

The controversy over *Natural Born Killers* also attracted renewed attention to Grisham's works and their content. Although he uses some violent scenarios, he has kept love scenes to a minimum. When reviewers taunted him about this position, he disregarded those comments and was candid about why he would not write anything he considered vulgar:

> Sex sells, but I really get irritated when I read a book and get the sense that the writer is using sex as a gimmick. Momma is still alive, so I can't write about sex. I don't know if I can do it very well anyway. It's a moral and literary choice. I'm not a guy who can write a book I'd be embarrassed for my kids to read in 15 years.[53]

Along with his decision not to write about sex, Grisham chooses not to use obscenities in his books. He believes a good story can be told without relying on the standard obscenities many other authors place throughout their books. In an interview with *Wineskins* magazine, Grisham says his choice to avoid unnecessary sex and distasteful language is based on his Baptist upbringing:

> When I started writing, I made the simple decision to keep it clean. The decision was based on my Christian faith and a certain lifestyle I'm trying to maintain, and I've never been tempted or pushed to write otherwise.[54]

Later in the same interview, Grisham further explains about his religious background and the impact it has had on his life. His growing-up years were centered around activities in the numerous small Baptist churches he attended. While moving from town to town, the family anchored themselves in the Baptist religion. When asked how the success of his books has affected his faith today, Grisham responded:

> Both my wife and I have middle-class backgrounds, and we've struggled with the overnight financial rewards of being a best-selling author. We give a lot of money to churches, missions, charities.[55]

## Repaying His Public

The donations Grisham mentioned in the *Wineskins* interview represent only a fraction of the author's willingness to repay people for their support. Among those who know him, he is almost as legendary for his generous nature as he is for his legal thrillers.

Part of his charitable contributions include his own time and sweat. Grisham has traveled to Brazil with his fellow church members to help build churches. On his initial journey, he learned about the lack of material possessions among the people in Brazil. It also reminded him of what he considers to be God's power:

> It was my first trip to a developing country, though, Brazil in many ways is thoroughly modern. It made me ashamed for all the material things I possess, and it showed me how little these things are worth. It also opened my eyes to the power of the gospel because for the first time I witnessed hundreds of people touched by it at the same time.[56]

Traveling to Brazil made an impression on Grisham, and he used the country as the main hiding place for his character, Patrick Lanigan, in *The Partner*. Readers learn about the people and landscape of Brazil through Patrick's appreciative perspective.

In *The Partner,* published in 1997, Grisham gives the reader another tale in which the characters are less important than the twists and turns in the plot. Although the characters do offer their thoughts and motivations, making them believable, the exciting part of the novel is how the puzzle pieces of Lanigan's past and present fit together.

*The Partner* adds a new dimension to Grisham's storytelling in that it almost seems as if he is role-playing, using Lanigan's character in a classic "what if" scenario. In one interview Grisham said the premise of the book, to take the money and run, is something nearly every lawyer fantasizes about: "*The Partner* is an old story. Lawyers dream of escaping, preferably with the money. I've known several who've tried it."[57]

*The Partner* is lighter in tone than many of Grisham's other books in which he tackles a social issue. However, even though the main character is granted freedom from prosecution, he is forced to return the cash he has stolen and he loses the profits he has made from that money. This moral lesson invites the reader to question greed in any form, even though compassion is evoked for Lanigan, who had matured in his inner growth.

In *The Street Lawyer*, published in 1998, Grisham's protagonist, Michael Brock, weighs his personal values as he tries to decide whether to stay with his law firm or to change careers. Eventually Brock chooses to leave the comfort and security of his firm to open a small practice aimed at helping street people. Before he leaves, though, he takes with him a file implicating his former firm in criminal acts. He then sets in motion a plan to sue them for millions of dollars.

## A Generous Heart

Some people would say the distaste for greed and subsequent moralizing in Grisham's later works mirror the author's much talked about internal character and generous nature. When one talks with those people who have known Grisham for years, the conversations begin to sound familiar. Words are repeated that emphasize his desire to remain unchanged despite his riches and celebrity.

Donald Zacharias, president emeritus of Mississippi State University, has been a friend of Grisham's for nearly twelve years. His description of the famous novelist has nothing to do with fame: "John is one of the most sincere and humble men I've ever met. Generous. With John, what you see is what you get."[58]

Zacharias has had the pleasure of watching Grisham's rise to success from the first novel to the lengthy list of books, tapes,

*Grisham confided in Donald Zacharias (left) about his hobby of writing. Zacharias encouraged Grisham to continue writing and told him that the university would display his notes and manuscript papers after he was published.*

and movies of today. In the early years, when Grisham was still writing *A Time to Kill* in morning sessions before court, he confided his hobby to Zacharias. The older man encouraged the young writer and told him that the university would be pleased to display his notes and manuscript papers after he became published. The promise was sealed on a handshake, and today MSU's Mitchell Memorial Library holds the special collection of John Grisham papers, consisting of nearly a decade of work.

The character traits Zacharias noticed about Grisham are the same ones that draw people each year to a bookstore in Blytheville, Arkansas. Bookstore owner Mary Gay Shipley even changed the bookstore's name to "That Bookstore in Blytheville" because everyone who returned for an autograph called it by that name. This store was the first to offer Grisham a public signing when *A Time to Kill* was newly published, and he never forgets to come back to Blytheville for a yearly book signing. The best-selling author is respected for his loyalty to these patrons who return each year when a new Grisham novel is released.

John Grisham is well loved by these people who travel from cities in Arkansas, Missouri, Louisiana, Mississippi, and Tennessee to talk with him while he signs their books. Even though he is a man who savors his privacy, here he enjoys visiting with old friends and even a few family members. At one book signing a lady approached his table and announced to those standing near her: "I'm his cousin. Actually, he's my husband's 'little' cousin. I'm good friends with his momma, and I took care of him when he was little—got him out of a lot of trouble." [59]

Throughout these sessions John Grisham is animated, making time for everyone in line, and he says a little something to each fan. At the same signing that his cousin attended, another woman drove five hours to see him and brought her high school writer's club with her. Grisham was happy to offer a little advice on writing to the students. "Take as many writing classes as you can," he advised. "Work on technical stuff, on grammar and vocabulary. And just keep writing." [60]

John has not only given his time away by signing books and offering encouragement to writers, he has also been featured as a commencement speaker for graduates of Mississippi State University. Speaking to a crowd of 1992 graduates, he gave them this bit of insight into his own life and how they should learn to remain open-minded about life's many possibilities:

> When I sat out there fifteen years ago, I was rather smug and confident, perhaps even a little arrogant because I, at the age of twenty-two, had already figured out my life. . . . I had it all planned, and thank goodness it didn't work. . . . Life will present you with unexpected opportunities, and it will be up to you to take a chance, to be bold, to have faith and go for it. [61]

Returning often to MSU and inspiring new graduates underscores Grisham's continued interest in education. Another indication of his commitment to learning was the establishment of the John Grisham Master Teacher Awards. Each year he donates a large monetary gift to honor five outstanding teachers at Mississippi State University who encourage students to learn as much as possible while in their classrooms.

*Grisham respectfully returns to bookstores to sign new releases of his novels for his loyal fans.*

## Back to Business

Grisham would like to be remembered as a positive element in Mississippi's history of literature and famous authors. He satisfied part of that wish by financially rescuing the regional magazine *Oxford American*. On another occasion, when money was needed for preservation of William Faulkner's home, known as Rowan Oak, Grisham made a generous contribution.

Grisham wants to continue his tradition of turning out a book a year and sees no need to negotiate new contract terms, as some writers have chosen to do. Stephen King, a famous writer of horror fiction, recently agreed to accept lower advances from publishers in favor of greater long-term profits. Grisham, however, already considers the large advances to be part of the profit-sharing arrangement:

> I think you reach a point with advances when it is a profit-sharing deal. When you start talking about the money that

is paid to me and to [Tom] Clancy and to [Stephen] King and to [Michael] Crichton and maybe even to Danielle [Steele]—I think those are the top five—in my opinion, it's profit sharing. The writer gets to make X number of dollars and the publisher makes X number of dollars.[62]

There are many writers, not in the top five Grisham mentions, who strongly believe that his idea of profit sharing does not help them. Authors who have solid audiences, but not the millions of fans Grisham has, are increasingly being edged out of the publishing fields. Publishers are not able to spend money promoting new authors because they have drained their bank accounts by paying large advances to a few guaranteed moneymakers. Most publishers simply do not have much room in their budgets to take chances on new or lesser-known authors.

Many publishers, editors, and writers in the literary world wonder about the future of their industry because of the phenomenon associated with writers such as Grisham. They worry that the choices being offered to readers are being limited by the pressure huge advances are putting on smaller publishers. Yet many readers seem content to keep making Grisham number one on their book-buying lists.

Bookstore owners see things differently. They believe that authors like Grisham not only help their incomes but also encourage many people to read who might not have read in years. Mary Gay Shipley says that she has had lots of customers tell her

## John Grisham's Ford County

Grisham hoped to create a little part of Mississippi history for himself with the invention of fictional Ford County, which served as the setting for some of his novels. Grisham took this cue from William Faulkner, a fellow Mississippi author who also created a fictional town for his stories.

In one portion of Grisham's 1992 commencement address at Mississippi State University, he gives a little insight into his perception of the fictional small town he calls Ford County: "It could be Starkville or Oxford, Ripley or West Point, Kosciusko or Brookhaven. You know the town because you've lived there."

*Wanting to be remembered as a positive element in Mississippi's history, Grisham contributed a generous amount of money for the preservation of Rowan Oak, the home of William Faulkner (pictured with his wife Estelle).*

that their relatives who have not read since high school are picking up a Grisham novel and reading it. She believes these people are enjoying an activity they used to associate with the pain of homework. "He's made a lot of people realize that reading can be fun,"[63] she says.

Bob Wietrak, vice president of merchandising for Barnes & Noble, believes that Grisham has actually increased the sales of other books as well. He says that 25 percent of customers who buy a newly released Grisham hardcover also purchase at least one other book before leaving the store:

> The first day his books are on sale, everyone is in the store buying the book. . . . While we depend on bestsellers to make up only 3%–4% of our weekly sales, Grisham is wonderful because he brings people into the store to buy other books.[64]

Considering that Grisham is so in favor of reading and education, this news from booksellers is quite a tribute to a man whose
legislative years were marked by his support of the BEST legislation. Anything he can do to encourage young people to read
is important to him.

## His Love of Baseball

Grisham's books still occupy best-seller lists, and movies based
on those books continue to reach millions of viewers. Even so,
Grisham has other high priorities. Regardless of the influence
his name still has on the publishing industry, Grisham's true
love remains baseball.

He offers himself wholly only to two groups of people—his
family, of course, and the Little League teams he coaches. When
the Charlottesville community he lives in needed a good baseball facility, Grisham paid for and helped build six fields for the
teams to practice on and play their games. Now he serves as
commissioner and ground crew, spending a great deal of time

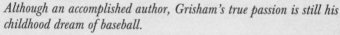

*Although an accomplished author, Grisham's true passion is still his
childhood dream of baseball.*

there. "I go to the ball field every afternoon and cut the grass, drag the dirt infield and put the chalk down for games," he says. "That thing is almost a full-time job."[65]

Although the ball field is a lot of work, Grisham has returned to his favorite element: each day living a part of his childhood dream. But his generosity toward the Little Leaguers did not stop with building and maintaining the fields.

During the spring of 1998, Grisham gathered his young ball players together and escorted them to Jacksonville, Florida, for their own version of spring training. He paid for all the players' travel expenses and gave them the thrill of their lives.

Although he has a big heart when it comes to the kids, he has a harder edge when dealing with the players' overbearing parents. "Every kid plays in every game. In fact, our league has a mandatory play rule," he says. "I ignore parents. If they gripe and complain, I invite them to take their precious bundle elsewhere."[66]

While Grisham's love of baseball continues to weave itself throughout his life, he is thankful for his decade of success as a novelist. Because of his celebrity status he has had to make some sacrifices, and yet he has shared his benefits with many others. In the world of books he might be considered a phenomenon, but in the world he calls home, Grisham will always remain a simple, honorable man.

# Notes

---

## Introduction: Superstar Novelist

1. Ted Conley, interview by author, Allen, Texas, August 21, 1998.
2. Quoted in Ann Oldenberg, "A Time for Grisham," *USA Today*, June 2, 1994, p. 1D.

## Chapter 1: Childhood Dreams

3. Quoted in Sammy McDavid, "A Time to Write," *Alumnus*, Winter 1990. Also available from http://www.msstate.edu/grisham, p. 2.
4. Quoted in "Profile," Hall of Arts website, available from http://www.achievement.org/autodoc/page/grisObio-1, p. 4.
5. Quoted in "Profile," p. 1.
6. Quoted in "Profile," p. 1.
7. John Grisham, "Journey's End," *Alumnus*, Winter 1995, available from http://www.msstate.edu/grisham, p. 2.
8. Quoted in Grisham, "Journey's End," *Alumnus*, p. 3.

## Chapter 2: Building a Legal and Political Career

9. Quoted in McDavid, "A Time to Write," *Alumnus*, p. 2.
10. Quoted in McDavid, "A Time to Write," *Alumnus*, p. 3.
11. Quoted in Robin Street, "Fast Track to Fame, Fortune," *Clarion-Ledger*, April 15, 1991, p. 2D.
12. Quoted in McDavid, "A Time to Write," *Alumnus*, p. 3.
13. Quoted in Mary Beth Pringle, *John Grisham: A Critical Companion*. Westport, CT: Greenwood Press, 1997, p. 2.
14. Scott Ross, interview by author, West Point, Mississippi, August 25, 1998.

15. John Grisham to Anthony Greene, February 28, 1987, John Grisham Papers, Mississippi State University Mitchell Memorial Library.

16. Ross interview.

## Chapter 3: An Inspired Writer

17. Quoted in Pringle, *John Grisham,* p. 2.

18. Quoted in "Profile," p. 3.

19. Quoted in "Profile," p. 3.

20. Quote on display, John Grisham Room, Mississippi State University Mitchell Memorial Library.

21. T. R. Pearson, "The Runaway Writer," *Harper's Bazaar,* March 1996, p. 326.

22. Quoted in Jesse Kornbluth, "Hot Picks," *Books-A-Million,* 1996, available from http://www.booksamillion.com/cat/id/grisham/interview1.html, p. 2.

23. Quoted in McDavid, "A Time to Write," *Alumnus,* p. 4.

24. Quoted in McDavid, "A Time to Write," *Alumnus,* p. 3.

25. Quoted in McDavid, "A Time to Write," *Alumnus,* p. 3.

26. Quoted in Street, "Fast Track to Fame, Fortune," *Clarion-Ledger,* p. 2D.

27. Quoted in Street, "Fast Track to Fame, Fortune," *Clarion-Ledger,* p. 2D.

28. Quoted in McDavid, "A Time to Write," *Alumnus,* p. 4.

29. Quoted in McDavid, "A Time to Write," *Alumnus,* p. 4.

30. Quoted in *Pen World,* January/February 1992.

31. Quoted in Frederic Koeppel, "Bestseller!" *Commercial Appeal,* May 26, 1991, p. G1.

32. Pringle, *John Grisham,* p. 43.

33. Quoted in Pringle, *John Grisham,* p. 43.

34. Pringle, *John Grisham,* p. 60.

35. Quoted in *Detroit News,* March 3, 1993.

## Chapter 4: A Publishing Phenomenon

36. Quoted in Don O'Briant, "The Grisham Brief," *Atlanta Journal-Constitution,* March 7, 1993, p. N1.

37. Pringle, *John Grisham,* p. 75.

38. Quoted in *Entertainment Weekly,* April 1, 1994.

39. Quoted in Lawrence Goodrich, "A Race Against a Mississippi Execution," *Christian Science Monitor,* June 10, 1994, p. 14.

40. Quoted in Oldenburg, "A Time for Grisham," p. 1D.

41. Quoted in Billy Watkins, "Grisham Talks," *Clarion-Ledger,* April 30, 1995, p. 1C.

42. Quoted in O'Briant, "The Grisham Brief," p. N6.

43. Quoted in O'Briant, "The Grisham Brief," p. N6.

44. Quoted in Watkins, "Grisham Talks," p. 1C.

45. Quoted in Katy Kelly, "Grisham's Smoking Jury," *USA Today,* September 8, 1997, available fromhttp://www.usatoday.com/ life/enter/book/leb371.htm, p.1.

46. Quoted in Lynn Elber, "John Grisham," *Daily Journal View Magazine,* August 20, 1995, p. 9G.

47. Quoted in Matthew Flamm, "A Time to Press Charges," *Entertainment Weekly,* September 27, 1996, p. 69.

## Chapter 5: Back to the Basics

48. Quoted in Jeff Zaleski, "The Grisham Business," *Publisher's Weekly,* January 19, 1998, p. 4.

49. Quoted in Zaleski, "The Grisham Business," p. 2.

50. Michael Shnayerson, "Natural Born Opponents," *Vanity Fair,* July 1996, p. 98.

51. Quoted in Shnayerson, "Natural Born Opponents," p. 98.

52. Quoted in Shnayerson, "Natural Born Opponents," p. 144.

53. Quoted in Koeppel, "Bestseller!" p. G2.

54. Quoted in Mike Cope, "Interview with John Grisham," *Wineskins,* vol. 2, no. 10, 1995, p. 6.

55. Quoted in Cope, "Interview with John Grisham," p. 7.

56. Quoted in Cope, "Interview with John Grisham," p. 7.

57. Quoted in Kornbluth, "Hot Picks," p. 3.

58. Donald Zacharias, interview by author, Starkville, Mississippi, August 12, 1998.

59. Quoted in Karen Knutson, "John Ray Grisham Jr.," *Arkansas Democrat Gazette,* April 4, 1993, p. 9D.

60. Quoted in Knutson, "John Ray Grisham Jr.," p. 9D.

61. John Grisham, "The Best Laid Plans," Mississippi State University summer commencement speech, 1992, available

from http://www.msstate.edu/grisham/Bestplans.html.

62. Quoted in Zaleski, "The Grisham Business," pp. 7–8.

63. Quoted in Elizabeth Bernstein, "He Creates New Readers," *Publisher's Weekly,* January 19, 1998, p. 251.

64. Quoted in Bernstein, "He Creates New Readers," p. 251.

65. Quoted in Kelly, "Grisham's Smoking Jury," p. 2.

66. Quoted in "Book Report Interview with John Grisham," *Book Report,* August 27, 1997, available from http://www.costco.com/pcc/art/top.draw/grisintv.htm, p. 4.

# Important Dates in the Life of John Grisham

**1955**
Born on February 8 in Jonesboro, Arkansas.

**1967**
Grisham family settles in Southaven, Mississippi.

**1977**
Graduates from Mississippi State University with a bachelor's degree in accounting.

**1981**
Graduates from the University of Mississippi with a degree in law; marries Renee Jones and moves back to Southaven to open his law practice.

**1983**
Elected to the Mississippi House of Representatives.

**1984**
Begins writing *A Time to Kill*.

**1987**
Finishes *A Time to Kill* and signs a contract with Jay Garon's literary agency.

**1988**
*A Time to Kill* is published by Wynwood Press.

**1991**
*The Firm* is published.

**1992**
*The Pelican Brief* is published.

**1993**
*The Client* is published.
**1994**
*The Chamber* is published.
**1995**
*The Rainmaker* is published; David Gernert becomes his new agent.
**1996**
*The Runaway Jury* is published.
**1997**
*The Partner* is published.
**1998**
*The Street Lawyer* is published.

# For Further Reading

John Grisham, "Journey's End," *Alumnus,* Winter 1995. Also available from http://www.msstate.edu/grisham. A personal essay by Grisham regarding his career and life choices.

Karen Knutson, "John Ray Grisham Jr.," *Arkansas Democrat Gazette,* April 4, 1993. Interview focusing on Grisham's personality and appeal to readers.

T. R. Pearson, "The Runaway Writer," *Harper's Bazaar,* March 1996. Profile of Grisham and his career through the eyes of a friend and fellow writer.

Mary Beth Pringle, *John Grisham: A Critical Companion.* Westport, CT: Greenwood Press, 1997. This is an in-depth look at Grisham's first seven novels regarding character, plot, theme, and writing style.

Robin Street, "Fast Track to Fame, Fortune," *Clarion-Ledger,* April 15, 1991. A lengthy article discussing Grisham's rapid rise to popularity and riches.

# Works Consulted

Elizabeth Bernstein, "He Creates New Readers," *Publisher's Weekly*, January 19, 1998.

"Book Report Interview with John Grisham," *Book Report,* August 27, 1997, available from http://www.costco.com/pcc/art/top.draw/grisintv.htm.

Mike Cope, "Interview with John Grisham," *Wineskins,* vol. 2, no. 10, 1995.

Lynn Elber, "John Grisham," *Daily Journal View Magazine,* August 20, 1995.

Matthew Flamm, "A Time to Press Charges," *Entertainment Weekly,* September 27, 1996.

Lawrence Goodrich, "A Race Against a Mississippi Execution," *Christian Science Monitor,* June 10, 1994.

John Grisham, "The Best Laid Plans," Mississippi State University summer commencement speech, 1992, available from http://www.msstate.edu/grisham/Bestplans.html.

Frederic Koeppel, "Bestseller!" *Commercial Appeal,* May 26, 1991.

Jesse Kornbluth, "Hot Picks," *Books-A-Million,* 1996, available from http://www.booksamillion.com/cat/id/grisham/interview1.html.

Katy Kelly, "Grisham's Smoking Jury," *USA* Today, September 8, 1997. Also available from http://www.usatoday.com/life/enter/book/leb371.htm.

Sammy McDavid, "A Time to Write," *Alumnus,* Winter 1990. Also available from http://www.msstate.edu/grisham.

Don O'Briant, "The Grisham Brief," *Atlanta Journal-Constitution,* March 7, 1993.

Ann Oldenberg, "A Time for Grisham," *USA Today,* June 2, 1994.

"Profile," Hall of Arts website, June 2, 1995, available from http://www.achievement.org/autodoc/page/grisObio-1.

Michael Shnayerson, "Natural Born Opponents," *Vanity Fair,* July 1996.

Billy Watkins, "Grisham Talks," *Clarion-Ledger,* April 30, 1995.

Jeff Zaleski, "The Grisham Business," *Publisher's Weekly,* January 19, 1998.

# Index

# Picture Credits

# About the Author

------------------------------------------------

Robyn M. Weaver is a writer, editor, and continuing education instructor at Texas Christian University. She travels across the country leading seminars about the mechanics of writing and also giving workshops on how to use writing to help heal emotional wounds.